21st
Century
Skills Library

COOL CAREERS

AUTO TECHNICIAN

KATIE MARSICO

Published in the United States of America by
Cherry Lake Publishing, Ann Arbor, Michigan
www.cherrylakepublishing.com

Content Adviser

John Walker, Automotive Technology Instructor, Hannibal Career & Technical Center,
Hannibal, Missouri

Credits

Photos: Cover and page 1, ©iStockphoto.com/blueflames; page 4, ©iStockphoto.
com/wbritten; page 6, ©lmdan/Dreamstime.com; page 9, ©iStockphoto.com/
sdominick; page 10, ©iStockphoto.com/petdcat; page 12, ©Sudheer Sakthan/
Shutterstock, Inc.; page 15, ©iStockphoto.com/gchutka; page 17, ©iStockphoto.
com/sumbul; pages 18, 20, and 28, ©iStockphoto.com/track5; page 23, ©Monkey
Business Images/Shutterstock, Inc.; page 24, ©iStockphoto.com/egdigital; page 27,
©iStockphoto.com/Juanmonino

Library of Congress Cataloging-in-Publication Data

Marsico, Katie, 1980-
  Auto technician/by Katie Marsico.
    p. cm.—(Cool careers)
  Includes bibliographical references and index.
  ISBN-13: 978-1-60279-937-0 (lib. bdg.)
  ISBN-10: 1-60279-937-7 (lib. bdg.)
  1. Automobile mechanics—Juvenile literature. 2. Automobiles—Maintenance and
repair—Vocational guidance—Juvenile literature. I. Title. II. Series.
  TL152.M274 2011
  629.28'7023—dc22   2010000687

Cherry Lake Publishing would like to acknowledge
the work of The Partnership for 21st Century Skills.
Please visit www.21stcenturyskills.org for more information.

Printed in the United States of America
Corporate Graphics Inc.
July 2010
CLFA07

COOL CAREERS

TABLE OF CONTENTS

CHAPTER ONE

SOLVING A MECHANICAL MYSTERY

Maria watched as her father tried to start the family van. He turned the key, but nothing happened. "Time to call a tow truck," he said. They would need to visit

Auto service technicians use their skills to keep vehicles running.

Mr. Jackson for help repairing the van. Mr. Jackson was the local auto service technician.

Maria and her father rode along with the driver in the tow truck. They took the van into the garage. "I have no idea what's wrong with it," Maria's father said to Mr. Jackson. Mr. Jackson and his assistants examined the van carefully. Maria and her father heard the whir and buzz of tools as they waited outside. Maria wondered if the auto service technician would be able to figure out what was wrong with the van. Finally, Mr. Jackson stepped outside to talk to them.

"I figured out what the problem is," he said. "The battery needs to be replaced. The whole job will cost about $100. Do you want me to go ahead and install it?" Maria's father said yes and thanked Mr. Jackson for his help. Soon, the car was fixed and ready to go.

Mr. Jackson showed Maria's father the bill. He explained the charges for the new part and the work he did. One of Mr. Jackson's assistants drove the van out of the garage. It was time to hit the road.

Maria discovered that auto service technicians have very important jobs. They are responsible for maintaining and repairing the vehicles that people rely on. Sometimes these workers are called auto mechanics. The term *auto service technician* is becoming more popular, though.

Auto service technicians need the skills to solve a variety of mechanical mysteries—and quickly! Like Maria's father, some people have trouble getting their cars to start. Some people hear strange sounds coming from the engine. Others have problems with their brakes.

Auto service technicians **diagnose** the cause of these problems. They use everything from wrenches to computers to figure out what is wrong. Then they make the necessary repairs. Auto service technicians also depend on feedback from customers. It is important for technicians to ask the

Special technicians work on race cars.

right questions. This helps them gather clues so they can decide what needs to be fixed.

Auto service technicians need to be able to communicate clearly and openly with their customers. They have to provide **estimates** of how much a job will cost and how long it will take. Owners want their vehicles back as soon as possible. They need to drive to work, school, and the many other places they go every day. Can you imagine life without your family car?

LEARNING & INNOVATION SKILLS

Most people think of auto service technicians as the people who work at garages and repair shops. But not all auto service technicians work at these places. Some of them have even found a way to combine their skills with their love of sports. These technicians work as members of pit crews.

Members of pit crews maintain and repair race cars. This can be a dangerous job. They often work next to racetracks and risk being hit by fast-moving vehicles. On the other hand, they tend to have higher pay than the average technician. They also get front-row seats to exciting races!

Auto service technicians encourage drivers to bring in their vehicles for routine maintenance. This is like taking your car for a yearly checkup. During routine maintenance, auto service technicians often **rotate** tires so they wear evenly. They also put fresh oil in the car. Oil helps the engine run smoothly and keeps it from getting too hot.

Many auto service technicians work on a variety of vehicles. Others only work with a particular make of car, such as Ford or Toyota. Some technicians only deal with certain parts of a car. For example, some focus on the body. Others handle problems inside of the car. They fix engines and **transmissions**. No matter what kind of work they do, auto service technicians usually have a busy schedule at the garage!

LIFE & CAREER SKILLS

In 2010, several models of Toyota vehicles were recalled. A problem with the cars caused them to accelerate out of control. Auto technicians at Toyota service centers were on the front lines of customer service. They were called upon to work extra hours to fix the problems and make sure customers' cars were safe to drive.

Some auto service technicians specialize in working on motorcycles.

CHAPTER TWO
A DAY AT THE GARAGE

Frankie sat in the garage's office with the phone held to his ear. He was on hold with the parts dealership. He had

A technician often spends time on the phone ordering parts or talking to customers.

called to see if they had a certain type of bumper in stock. A customer named Mrs. Davis had dented her rear bumper in a small accident. She wanted to replace it with a new one.

Frankie had promised to contact the parts dealership and see how much the bumper would cost. The saleswoman returned to the phone and told him that they had the bumper he needed. Its cost was $300. Frankie would also have to spend time painting and installing the bumper. The total cost of the repair would run Mrs. Davis about $700. Frankie knew that Mrs. Davis wanted her car back as soon as possible. He dialed her number right after he figured out the total cost.

"Should I go ahead and order the bumper?" he asked after explaining his estimate. "I can probably finish the job in a few days if I get the part this afternoon."

"That sounds great," answered Mrs. Davis. "Thanks for getting back to me so quickly!"

"No problem," replied Frankie. "I'll let you know when the car is ready to go." He hung up the phone and redialed the parts dealership to place the order. He could already tell it was going to be a busy morning.

Auto service technicians often have unpredictable schedules. They can get very busy when a lot of customers all need work done at the same time. Their schedules also depend on how big their garages are and how many other people work there.

Different kinds of jobs can also affect a technician's schedule. Some repairs take much longer than others. This means a technician's schedule can change from day to day. He might put in 30 hours one week and 80 hours the next. Many garages are also open evenings and weekends to fit into their customers' schedules.

Computers can help diagnose problems faster.

Auto service technicians usually complete many different tasks each day. They talk with customers and parts dealerships. They also do inspections and repairs. An auto service technician usually starts a shift by looking over his workload. Sometimes he might have a job from the day before that he still needs to finish.

He also has to make time to talk to new customers who bring their cars to the garage. Auto service technicians must ask detailed questions and pay careful attention to the answers. Sometimes customers have simple requests. They may just want a **tune-up** or an oil change.

The request can sometimes be more complex, though. A customer might know that her car is not working properly without understanding why. The auto service technician must identify the reason. First, he tries to figure out how long the customer has been having car problems. Then he asks the customer if she notices anything unusual about the way her vehicle is running. Is it making odd noises? When was the car's last routine maintenance checkup?

An auto service technician thinks about the customer's answers as he takes a closer look at the vehicle. He relies on several different tools to help diagnose the exact cause of the trouble. He often raises the car on a **lift** so he can examine the bottom. He uses basic hand tools such as screwdrivers, pliers, and wrenches. He also uses special computers and **infrared** devices.

Soon, the technician diagnoses the problem. Then he figures out how to correct it. Sometimes he can make the repair in house. Garages with in-house machine shops have tools that can be used to cut and shape metal.

LIFE & CAREER SKILLS

Just because auto service technicians spend a lot of time working on cars doesn't mean they don't have to talk to people. In fact, men and women who enter this field would be lost if they couldn't speak to customers in a professional way. Customers are not always happy or grateful people. A technician sometimes needs to explain why a car requires a costly repair or why it has to stay in the shop for an extra day. This can make customers upset. Successful auto service technicians must know how to stay cool under pressure and help customers understand what is going on with their vehicles.

Other times, the technician may have to order parts from the dealerships that make and sell them. Either way, he contacts the customer first to let her know how much the

Calm and clear communication is necessary in order to get the job done.

repair will cost. The auto service technician begins work if she agrees to the estimate.

The work might involve anything from painting a bumper to fixing a **radiator** leak to replacing a spark plug. Such jobs are often messy. It is common for auto service technicians to handle greasy or dirty parts, so they wear washable uniforms and gloves. Some even put on goggles to keep metal scraps or oil from getting in their eyes. They understand that it is important to be safe in the garage.

It is important for auto service technicians to be polite and efficient. A technician must call the customer after he completes a job to let her know she can pick up her car. Then he must explain everything he did, what problems he ran into, and how he fixed them. He also fills out an invoice outlining the charges for the job. The workday ends when the auto service technician finally watches the last customer of the day drive away from the garage. Then it is time to put away tools and prepare for the next morning.

Auto repair shops often have room to work on several cars at once.

CHAPTER THREE
BECOMING AN AUTO SERVICE TECHNICIAN

Annie walked into her first class at the local **technical school**. She thought of her earliest memories

Becoming a good auto service technician requires knowledge and hands-on experience.

of helping her Uncle Matthew repair cars. Uncle Matthew was an auto service technician. Annie had decided at a young age that she wanted to do the same type of work when she grew up. Annie used to sit in the garage and hand her uncle tools as he tested and replaced parts. She enjoyed the idea of knowing how to fix something as big and fast as a car.

"Besides," Annie had thought as a little girl, "a job at a garage seems easy enough. Uncle Matthew says he didn't have to take many classes to become an auto service technician." Annie's uncle had learned most of his skills working as an **apprentice** for several years. After that, he had been hired by a big repair shop. He operated his own garage by the time Annie was born.

She had always dreamed of helping him run the family business. Uncle Matthew reminded Annie that training for a career as an auto service technician wasn't as easy as it seemed. He explained that technology was changing at an amazing rate. It was important for Annie to receive a good education. She needed to learn how to use the latest tools so she could work on newer cars.

"Vehicles nowadays have at least five onboard computers, usually more," Uncle Matthew said when Annie told him about her plans for the future. "Electronics affect everything from a car's brakes to its sound system to its transmission. You need to understand how all that equipment works in addition to basic auto mechanics."

He had recommended that Annie check out programs at nearby community colleges and trade and technical schools. She had followed his advice. Now it was her first day of classes. She couldn't wait to get started. She hoped that once she was finished she would be able to teach Uncle Matthew a thing or two about cars.

Training programs are a great way to get started as an auto service technician.

People who want to prepare for careers as auto service technicians have a few different options. A small number of people still break into the field without any formal education. They learn their skills from hands-on experience as apprentices.

Some high schools offer training programs, but a growing number of people prefer to continue their learning at community colleges and trade and technical schools. Their studies can last anywhere from 6 months to 2 years. Community colleges encourage students to also take courses in related subjects such as English, math, and computer science.

Part of an auto service technician's education takes place in a classroom. Some of it also occurs in garages. This allows students to apply their skills to real-life situations. How can you decide which school is right for you?

The National Automotive Technicians Education Foundation (NATEF) can help make your choice easier. NATEF certifies auto service technician training programs. In other words, they make sure schools meet the standards set by the auto industry. More than 2,250 programs in the United States are NATEF certified.

Auto service technicians can also take special classes and tests to receive National Institute for Automotive Service Excellence (ASE) certification. This helps them stand out in the field. ASE-certified technicians are sometimes able to advance in their careers more quickly than others.

LIFE & CAREER SKILLS

How can you start preparing for a career as an auto service technician while you're still in grade school? Start by talking to the staff at local repair shops. Ask your parents and older friends and relatives about how their cars work.

Being an auto service technician involves more than just understanding how cars work. People who have succeeded in this field are good at analyzing problems and thinking on their feet. Most also have strong reading, math, and computer skills. Do you fit this description?

Even these professionals do not usually start off running garages and shops. Many work as assistants to more established auto service technicians for a few years. Then they find higher-paying jobs as **journeymen** and journeywomen. Journeymen practice simple repairs and maintenance. They gain experience by taking on more and more difficult tasks. Auto service technicians can make anywhere from $9.56 to $28.71 per hour. Their earnings partially depend on which skills they have and how much professional training they have had.

Working with an experienced technician is one way to improve your skills.

Does it seem like becoming an auto service technician requires a lot of effort and planning? It can involve more work than most people think. It can be well worth it, though. Most experts believe opportunities will only continue to grow for people who enter this field.

CHAPTER FOUR
LOOKING TOWARD THE FUTURE

Tom could not wait to share the good news with his family. His boss at the garage had just told him that he would

More cars with more advanced technology means more auto service technicians will be needed.

be receiving a raise. This would bring his salary to about $20 an hour. Tom enjoyed working as an auto service technician. He had attended classes at his high school and local community college to strengthen his technical skills. He had even become ASE certified. Now he would be earning more money with each paycheck.

"What a wonderful surprise," Tom's wife said when he told her about his raise. "You must be happy to see all your efforts pay off. Maybe one day you'll even be in charge of the entire garage!"

"I hope so," replied Tom. "I definitely think I picked the right career. I'm pretty sure the opportunities will keep coming if I keep taking classes to learn about the latest auto technology."

Tom was correct. The U.S. Department of Labor estimates that employment opportunities for auto service technicians will increase by about 5 percent between 2008 and 2018. Experts believe this for several reasons.

First, the number of vehicles being driven in the United States continues to rise. This means more auto service technicians will be needed to perform maintenance tasks and repairs. In addition, automakers are building vehicles to last longer. Drivers will rely on professionals to help them care for this new and advanced technology.

Auto service technicians will still have to prove themselves in order to win the best jobs. Many employers will want to hire workers with specialized training. They will also want people who are familiar with computers and the other fast-paced changes that are shaping the auto industry. Auto service technicians who are not ASE certified or who do not have a formal education may find it harder to compete.

21ST CENTURY CONTENT

Many people today want to take better care of the environment. This provides new opportunities for auto service technicians. For example, more and more people are driving hybrid cars. These people will need the help of auto service technicians who can work on this kind of vehicle.

Hybrid cars run on both gas-powered engines and electric motors. This lowers the amount of air pollution from burning fuel. The demand for auto service technicians who specialize in hybrid cars will continue to grow as drivers look for new ways to save gas and protect the environment.

Even experienced technicians take classes to stay up to date on new technology.

The future is sure to be exciting for auto service technicians. Vehicles are changing rapidly as technology continues to advance. People rely on their cars to get around and enjoy their lives. There will always be a demand for professionals who care for vehicles. Do you see yourself wearing an auto service technician's uniform one day?

Being an auto service technician can be a challenging and rewarding career.

SOME WELL-KNOWN ORGANIZATIONS FOR AUTO SERVICE TECHNICIANS

Automotive Service Association (ASA)

PO Box 929
Bedford, TX 76095-0929
800/272-7467
www.asashop.org
This trade association was formed in 1951. It offers professional services to owners and managers of automotive repair and maintenance businesses. Conventions, training opportunities, and a variety of publications are a few examples of member benefits.

National Automotive Technicians Education Foundation (NATEF)

101 Blue Seal Drive SE, Suite 101
Leesburg, VA 20175
703/669-6650
www.natef.org
This organization was founded in 1983. It evaluates and certifies training programs for auto service technicians.

The National Institute for Automotive Service Excellence (ASE)

(Same mailing address as the NATEF)
703/669-6600
www.ase.com
This organization is affiliated with the NATEF. It was established in 1972 to raise professional standards among auto service technicians. People can receive ASE certification in various specialties by passing exams.

GLOSSARY

apprentice (uh-PREN-tuhss) someone who works for an expert to learn a trade

diagnose (dye-ig-NOHSS) to determine the cause of a problem

estimates (ESS-tuh-muhts) approximate calculations of how much something will cost

infrared (in-fruh-RED) relating to a certain range of invisible radiation wavelengths

journeymen (JUHR-nee-men) craftsmen who have completed an apprenticeship; craftswomen who match this description are referred to as journeywomen

lift (LIFT) a machine used to raise a car into the air so its bottom and interior can be viewed more clearly

radiator (RAY-dee-ay-tuhr) the part of an automobile that emits heat

rotate (ROE-tayt) turn

technical school (TEK-nih-kuhl SKOOL) a school that offers courses and training to prepare students for mechanical and industrial careers

transmissions (trans-MIH-shuhnz) systems of parts, including gears, that send power from a car's engine to its axle

tune-up (TOON-uhp) regular maintenance performed on an automobile's engine

FOR MORE INFORMATION

BOOKS

Eason, Sarah. *How Does a Car Work?* New York: Gareth Stevens Publishing, 2010.

Hammond, Richard. *Car Science*. New York: DK Publishing, 2008.

Jozefowicz, Chris. *Auto Technician*. Pleasantville, NY: Gareth Stevens Publishing, 2010.

WEB SITES

Guide to Career Education: Automotive Technician
www.guidetocareereducation.com/careers/automotive-technician
Check out this Web page for a closer look at automotive careers, including the various fields auto service technicians can specialize in.

United States Department of Labor: Bureau of Labor Statistics—Automotive Mechanic
www.bls.gov/k12/build02.htm
Scan this site for information related to career training, salaries, and an overview of what auto technicians do.

INDEX

ABOUT THE AUTHOR

Katie Marsico has written more than 60 books for young readers. She is by no means an expert on cars, which is why she has such great respect for her family's auto technician, Nick.